A PIECE OF
THE MOON WORLD

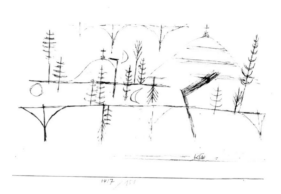

Paul Klee in Texas Collections

A PIECE OF
THE MOON WORLD

Paul Klee in Texas Collections

Foreword by
Dominique de Menil

Essay by
Ileana Marcoulesco

Introduction by
Susan Davidson

THE MENIL COLLECTION

1995

This exhibition catalogue was made possible
by the generous support of the
Clarence Foundation, Switzerland and
an anonymous donor

Additional support has been received from
Sulzermedica USA, Inc. and
Union Bank of Switzerland

Exhibition dates: March 9 to June 5, 1994

Cover: *Gaze of Silence,* 1932, [pl. 26]
Fig. 1: *Landscape,* 1917
Frontispiece: Josef Albers, photograph of Paul Klee, 1929
Back Cover: Josef Albers, photograph of Paul Klee, 1929

LIBRARY OF CONGRESS CATALOGING-IN-PUBLICATION DATA
Klee, Paul, 1879–1940.
    A piece of the moon world : Paul Klee in Texas collections /
introduction by Susan Davidson ; essay by Ileana Marcoulesco.
        p.   cm.
    Exhibition dates : March 9 to June 5, 1994 at the Menil
Collection, Houston.
    Includes bibliographical references.
    ISBN 0-939594-31-5
    1. Klee, Paul, 1879–1940 – Exhibitions.   2. Art – Texas – Houston –
Exhibitions.   3. Menil Collection (Houston, Tex.) – Exhibitions.
4. Art – Collectors and collecting – Texas.   I. Menil Collection
(Houston, Tex.)   II. Title
N6888.K55A4 1994
759.9494 – dc20   94-4876
                                                                          CIP

Printed in the Federal Republic of Germany.

Contents

Acknowledgments

IN PREPARING THE EXHIBITION, I had the pleasure of working with several people. Chief among these are Stefan Frey of the Paul Klee Foundation, who willingly shared his vast knowledge about Paul Klee and supplied invaluable research. Lyle Williams, assistant curator at the McNay Art Museum, Barry Walker, curator at The Museum of Fine Arts, Houston, and Joeliene Magoto, director of the Old Jail Art Center in Albany, enthusiastically embraced the exhibition and assisted with loans. In addition, Lisa Doherty, Barbara Hendry, Heather Hornbuckle, Wynne Phelan, and Francis Trevino deserve acknowledgment.

The support of my colleagues at The Menil Collection has been invaluable. Dominique de Menil's vision guided all aspects of the exhibition. Paul Winkler, director, and Walter Hopps, consulting curator, offered valued criticism and encouragement. Geraldine Aramanda, Julie Bakke, Deborah Brauer, Gayle de Gregori, Elizabeth Lunning, and William Steen contributed greatly to the exhibition's organization and installation and Don Quaintance designed the exhibition catalogue.

The realization of the catalogue owes much to an anonymous donor, whose love for Paul Klee's work enticed her to make the initial donation to its production. A significant grant was received from the Clarence Foundation, Switzerland. Alfred Killias, Swiss Consul General of Houston, offered welcomed guidance in securing additional contributions. I am grateful to T.C. Selman II, group vice president of Sulzermedica USA, and Alfred Imholz, first vice president of the Union Bank of Switzerland, who facilitated contributions from their respective organizations.

The success of any exhibition depends in large part on its lenders. I am especially indebted to the individuals and institutions listed below without whose generosity the exhibition could not have occurred.

—Susan Davidson

LENDERS TO THE EXHIBITION

Janie C. Lee
McNay Art Museum, San Antonio
Christophe de Menil
The Menil Collection, Houston
The Museum of Fine Arts, Houston

Old Jail Art Center, Albany, Texas
Francesco Pellizzi
R.L.B. Tobin
Mr. and Mrs. James M. Vaughn, Jr.
and several anonymous lenders

Foreword

THIS SHOW, MODEST IN SIZE BUT REPLETE WITH TREASURES, offers an opportunity to gain deeper insight into the genius of Paul Klee.

Who better than Klee himself to open the door of our intelligence and sensitivity toward his work.

Paul Klee wrote: "The heart must do its work undisturbed by the reflective consciousness."[1] He said also: "Still more important than the primary vision remains the reality of form for which the true artist must struggle again and again. Form often develops of its own free will and strives to dominate with ever-increasing authority. Only with great effort can the artist control it. This is a real fight, demanding strength and sound nerves. For a long time, I could work but little, because the discord between first vision and ultimate expression was too strong to be overcome. I had to wait and wait—this was most difficult. Although I suffered, I always preferred doing nothing until the purity of form was assured and work forced itself upon me."[2]

May this catalogue let us into the *Gaze of Silence.*

—Dominique de Menil

1. Karl Nierendorf, "Notes on Klee," *Paul Klee, Paintings, Watercolors, 1913 to 1939.* New York, 1941, 25.

2. "Notes on Klee," 25–26.

Introduction

THE PREMISE FOR THIS EXHIBITION WAS SIMPLE: to choose an artist who is well represented within The Menil Collection and to investigate how he was collected within a defined area—in this case, the state of Texas. After careful investigation, twenty-eight works in all media belonging to private collectors and public institutions throughout the state were identified in addition to the twenty-four works already at the Menil.[1] Klee's art has been collected consistently in Texas since the 1930s, although he was the recipient of only one solo exhibition. Organized by the Committee on Contemporary Art and spearheaded by Dominique de Menil's enthusiasm for his work, "Paul Klee Paintings and Watercolors," an exhibition of forty paintings and works on paper, was held at the Museum of Fine Arts, Houston, in 1960. Now, more than thirty-four years later, "A Piece of the Moon World: Paul Klee in Texas Collections" brings together a selection of thirty-four works by Klee, having as its nucleus those works collected since 1955 by Dominique de Menil and her late husband, John de Menil.

The intelligent nature of Klee's work offers what Dominique de Menil has often called "enchantment with erudition." The de Menils purchased their first Klee drawing, *Austere Rock Formation* (fig. 2), in 1955. New Klee pictures were acquired in New York and Paris, where they frequented the galleries that represented Klee's work, such as Saidenberg, World House, Nierendorf, and New Art galleries in New York and Heinz Berggruen's gallery in Paris. Their Klee collection grew fairly consistently by two to four works every year for the next ten years, after which pictures were added more sporadically.[2] The last Klee works to enter their collection—*Analysis of a Moment* (pl. 21), *Blossoms in their Place* (pl. 24), and an original edition of Klee's *Pedagogical Sketchbook*, 1925—did so within the last fifteen years, when the museum which now houses their art collection was being established. A nonencyclopedic approach, true of all areas of The Menil Collection from prehistoric to contemporary art, applies to the Klee works. The de Menils never intended to acquire the full spectrum of Klee's styles and techniques.

fig. 2 *Austere Rock Formation,* 1927

Although he never traveled to America, Klee enjoyed a widespread reputation here during his lifetime. Along with Wassily Kandinsky, he represented the vanguard of German art in America through the collective effort of a few pioneers. Katherine S. Dreier was the first to exhibit his work in a group show in 1921, and she organized Klee's first solo exhibition in America three years later.[3] But it was the effort of Galka Scheyer that was in large measure responsible for distributing Klee's art across the United States. Scheyer, a former Bauhaus pupil, moved here in 1924 and worked primarily as a self-appointed ambassador for her *Blue Four* friends (Lyonel Feininger, Alexei von Jawlensky, Kandinsky, and Klee), advancing their careers through exhibitions and lectures until her death in 1945. Her estate, including fifty-six Klee paintings and works on paper, was bequeathed to the Pasadena Museum of Art, now the Norton Simon Museum. The Baroness Hilla von Rebay, who emigrated to the United States in 1927, laid the foundations of the Solomon R. Guggenheim Museum's Klee collection. Although her interest was primarily in non-objective art, Rebay maintained a lifelong commitment to Klee; four of the seventy-seven Klee works in the Guggenheim were acquired on her advice. Klee's presence in the United States was cemented in 1930 when he became the first living European painter to receive a one-person exhibition at the newly opened

Museum of Modern Art in New York. The exhibition (sixty-three pictures executed between 1919 and 1930) demonstrated to American audiences Klee's extraordinary productivity as well as his technical and stylistic range.[4]

The first Klee artworks to reach Texas were brought here by the Houston philanthropist Ima Hogg, returning from one of her frequent trips to Europe. Although she did not generally collect European avant-garde art, it is not surprising that Ima Hogg developed an interest in Klee, who shared her passion for music (it is not known whether they had occasion to meet). Hogg was intrigued when one afternoon in 1930 she purchased three choice works—a 1920 lithograph, *Park*, and two watercolors, *Marjamshausen* (pl. 15) and *Sel*, 1929, from Galerie Moeller in Berlin. The drawings did not stay long in her collection; in 1939 they were among the first of many gifts to The Museum of Fine Arts, Houston. The fourth work comprising that institution's Klee holdings, *Still Life in Brown* (pl. 30), was given to the museum in 1963 by Mr. and Mrs. Pierre Schlumberger.

Texans had to wait until after World War II to become reacquainted with Klee's work. Two of Klee's European gallery dealers who had emigrated to America during the war—Karl Nierendorf and Curt Valentin with his Buchholz Gallery—did a great deal throughout the 1940s and 1950s to present Klee's art to the American public, in general, and Texans, in particular. Nierendorf's clientele included the anonymous donor of the 1924 *Murder with a Sun Umbrella, A Scherzo* to the Fort Worth Art Association, now the Fort Worth Museum of Modern Art. Bill Bomar, a north Texas artist, also frequented Nierendorf's gallery, where he developed an affinity for Klee's painting. *Way into the Blue* (pl. 28), which Bomar purchased at a precocious age while living in New York, resonates with his own aesthetic concerns. This work was bequeathed upon his death in 1991 to the Old Jail Art Center, which he and his cousin had founded in their hometown of Albany, Texas.

The city of San Antonio has produced several Klee collectors, all centered around the collecting activities of Marion Koogler McNay. McNay's interest in Klee developed out of her regard for German Expressionism. She was undoubtedly introduced to Klee by the Los Angeles art dealer Dalzell Hatfield (her trusted friend and almost exclusive dealer), who, through his association with Scheyer, served as Klee's representative outside New York. Oddly, McNay did not acquire any Klees from Hatfield, waiting until 1950, the last year of her life, to purchase *On the River* (pl. 34) from Valentin's Buchholz Gallery. Nonetheless, the San Antonio attorney Sylvan Lang and his wife, Mary, who were close friends of McNay's,[5] purchased Untitled *(Vegetation in Rejuvenation)* (pl. 7) from Hatfield in 1960, after acquiring their first ink drawing, *The Vocalist* (pl. 6), the previous year from the Saidenberg Gallery. Robert L.

B. Tobin, currently a trustee of the McNay Art Museum, has focused his collecting on stage and costume design, and his love for the theater is expressed in Klee's *House of the Opera Buffa* (pl. 13). Klee was among the first artists Tobin, like many Texas collectors, began acquiring. *Short Story in Secret Code* (pl. 33) was purchased from the Saidenberg Gallery over thirty years ago, and to date, Tobin has acquired a number of other examples, making him, after the de Menils, the second largest Klee collector in the state.

"A PIECE OF THE MOON WORLD: PAUL KLEE IN TEXAS COLLECTIONS" spans Klee's entire career but does not pretend to be an exhaustive survey.[6] For the most part, the works included here are abstract rather than figurative. There are a number of landscapes—both urban and pastoral—as well as works devoted to botanical, architectural, and musical themes. Representations of some of the many different techniques Klee invented are also included: gradations, pointillism, and priming and scratching methods, to name a few. Viewed together, Klee's pictures form a lexicon of his artistic expression, encompassing the complexity of his pictorial vocabulary as well as the diversity and multidimensionality of his subjects and styles.[7] The selection at hand introduces witty associations and establishes a harmony which only an artist of Klee's imagination could achieve.

—Susan Davidson

NOTES

1. This does not include the eight known works once in private Texas collections that have been either sold at auction, given to institutions outside of Texas, or presented to people living outside the state.

2. Several Klee works on paper acquired by the de Menils were presented as gifts to either friends or family members; three of these are included in this exhibition.

3. "Société Anonyme Exhibition 14," March 15-April 12, 1921, and "Paul Klee," January 7-February 7, 1924 at the Société Anonyme (Heckscher Building), New York.

4. I am indebted to Carolyn Lachner, "Klee in America" in *Paul Klee*, The Museum of Modern Art, 1987, 83-111 and Lisa Dennison, "Introduction" in *Paul Klee at the Guggenheim*

Museum , New York, 1993, 9-17, for these historical data.

5. The Langs' collection of more than seventy works, ranging from Henry Moore sculpture to American regionalism, was bequeathed to the McNay Art Museum in 1973.

6. The decision was made to exclude Klee's graphic work from the exhibition; this includes the single etching in a Texas collection (*Comedian*, 1904, at the Archer M. Huntington Art Gallery of The University of Texas at Austin) and seven lithographs held both privately and publicly within the state. In addition, conservation considerations prohibited several works from being included in this presentation.

7. Dennison, 10.

Unclassifiable Klee

> "In immanence, I am ungraspable."
> —Paul Klee, *Diaries*

> Art is not construction, artifice, industrious relationship to a space or to an exterior world. It is really the "unarticulated cry" of which Hermes Trismegistus spoke, "that appeared to be the voice of light itself."
> —Maurice Merleau-Ponty, *L'œil et l'esprit*

IN TODAY'S CACOPHONIC ORCHESTRATION OF THE ART WORLD, Paul Klee does not shock anymore, nor did he rely on shock values in his time. He made his way in the world tacitly, without fanfare, and without great imbalance or dramatic shifts in manner. It is hard to pinpoint well-defined periods in his style, for they overlap constantly. He invented new techniques as he went, out of inner necessity, not to shake the world. His "revolution" was in fact one of strict interiority, even as he progressed in abstraction and self-understanding.

Paul Klee was a multifaceted personality and an artist of indisputable versatility. His interests for the purely plastic or graphic ranged from calligraphy, ideograms, pictograms, systems of encoding and decoding, alphabets, and semiotics to music theory and some esoteric fields of mathematics. He was not indifferent to literature or to history: from Novalis to Montezuma, he often illustrated cultural and historical themes. He was interested in other races and their physiognomies, especially the blacks and the Chinese.

In spite of the variation of styles, Klee's oeuvre possesses a monolithic inner structure, a template so original that it belies influences or rather affirms the perfect blend of all the influences he absorbed. He achieved such a degree of assimilation of external models that it is almost impossible to rank his work within established categories or trends. A rare feature, in which he is possibly only Picasso's equal, is the ease and grace with which he traverses the gap between form and content: he rides continuously on the artistic Möbius strip, creating surreptitious passages between the inside and the outside, form and emotion, immanence and transcendence.

◆ ◆ ◆

BORN IN DECEMBER OF 1879 IN SWITZERLAND, Klee spent almost half of his life in Germany, near Munich, and returned to his homeland in 1933, where he died in 1940. He was trained as a violinist and a painter. Mostly he built himself, step by step, into an original artist by devising new techniques and styles, by teaching and inventing as he went, by systematizing and testing his own intuitions.

An early influence was Italy, which he visited in 1901. The frescoes at Pompeii, the Byzantine mosaics, and the aquarium in Naples may explain, to some extent, Klee's early preference for decorativism, the later reinvention of mosaiclike divisionism, and his lasting fondness for marine life.

Klee started his public shows as an Expressionist in the German tradition, having adopted the Gothic style of satirical etchings (1903–1905), but soon found his own voice. Above all chronological divisions in the unfolding of his creation, Klee discerned three *circles* or manners: the *outer circle,* comprising the early satirical sketches, still lifes, landscapes, and some portraits; the *middle circle,* containing architectural constructions and technical innovations, such as hatching and lace effects; finally, the *inner circle,* encompassing "magic geometries," works focused on the passage from the static to the dynamic, musical paintings, chromatic gradations, and the metaphysical portraits. There is definitely a progression in dynamism and poetic quality from the *outer* to the *inner circle.*

For those familiar only with the *middle* or *inner circle* of Klee's work, the early grotesque phase seems to have another paternity altogether. And, indeed, in his maturity Klee deviated from this manner in the direction of a conceptual inscription of ugliness. In his youth, Klee took a shot at hateful things with ugly means. Familiar with Gogol and Dostoyevsky, he did not mince his words when it came to expressing distaste, mockery, or disapproval. However, there was no "aesthetization of ugliness"; for all his capacity to transmit the shudder at the monstrous, the caricatures were still satires acceptable to the bourgeois. In his late years, however, horror was to be otherwise internalized and conveyed by "beautiful, symbolic means," achieving often tragic effects.

Speaking of *Threatening Head* (1905), one of his better known satirical etchings, Klee himself writes: "A thought more destructive than action. Pure negation as demon." Until about 1928, a diabolic incisiveness manifested itself in the angular, scratchy lines, and in the bellicose air imparted to the subjects of his caricatures.

Ugly also are the Giacometti-like figures that animate his illustrations to Voltaire's *Candide,* published in 1920: they look like improvisations of dancing puppets. Aversion for Leibnizian optimism? Resonance with Voltaire's bittersweet mockery of "the best of all possible worlds"? Sublimation of aggressive feelings and contradictory judgments? Some tragicomic heroes from this period resemble classical statues with mutilated limbs, in mock-heroic attitudes. Klee's wrath seems directed at postures of aggrandizement, at empty conventions, at lies and deceptions.

This perceptual "ugliness" usually conveys his irritation or mild disgust, when it is not his irrepressible laughter at the stupidity of a situation. "To emphasize only the beautiful seems to me to be like a mathematical system that only concerns itself with positive numbers," Klee wrote in his *Diary* of 1906.

In Klee's late years, we still encounter the old satire, albeit stylistically much simplified and more enigmatic. The mostly tragic hideousness of Klee's last works may in part be a result of his incurable illness,[1] of the despair that invaded him at the thought of the end. Yet it has a metaphysical dimension that remains enigmatic: without postulating some form of transcendence, the *inner circle* remains unfathomable.

Ugliness, thus, has two aesthetic registers in Klee. In the early stage (1903–1907) it was easy to understand for it espoused an expressionistic form: Klee admired and borrowed from Edvard Munch, Henri Toulouse-Lautrec, and Franz Marc, his colleague and friend in the *Blue Rider* group. The later stage of "ugliness" is totally different. It involves an intense, almost abyssal deepening of the shorthand of his mature style; the famous line becomes either thicker, spasmodic, or extremely wiry: the human faces become emaciated, reduced to an absolute minimum. In these works of the *inner circle*, his inimitable *synthesis of the figurative and the abstract* makes him even less liable to categorization, except on his own terms.

◆ ◆ ◆

IN 1904, AT THE PINAKOTHEK IN MUNICH, he saw the works of Blake, Beardsley, and Goya; in 1908, at the "Spring Secession" exhibition, Bonnard and van Gogh; and in Geneva, Corot. He made a slow transition towards modernity. In van Gogh, he recognized a genius of the expressive line, even while rejecting his pathos. As for the Impressionists, he considered the fragmentation of light their highest achievement.

He was already aware that his line was his most original possession and knew the reasons of his own discontent with naturalism. Prophetically, he wrote about the advent of modernism:

> A work of art goes beyond naturalism the instant the line enters in as an independent pictorial element, as in van Gogh's drawings and paintings, and in Ensor's graphics...In fact I am beginning to see a way to provide a place for my line. I am at last finding my way out of the dead end of ornamentation where I found myself one day in 1907.[2]

In 1911, Klee met Wassily Kandinsky and his wife Nina, through the *Blue Rider,* a fallout from the *NKV (Neue Künstlerische Vereinigung),* a cosmopolitan association of artists established in Bavaria a few years earlier. The friendship with the Kandinskys was to last a lifetime. The *Blue Rider* had helped channel the Russian artists toward abstraction. Moreover, Franz Marc, Braque, Arp, Derain, Kirchner, Nolde, and Picasso were all active associates in the club. They proved admirably receptive to all styles of art that were possessed of a certain innerness, self-reflection, and were open as well to "primitive" and "outsider art": medieval woodcuts, Asian and African masks, the art of children and of the insane. The same movement brought together painters and modernist musicians—Schönberg, Alban Berg, Hindemith, Webern—all bent upon cross-experiments between music and painting.

By 1912, Kandinsky had arrived at a crystallized expression of his own theories on art and published an influential philosophical manifesto, *Concerning the Spiritual in Art* (this, four years before he started painting according to his own doctrine). In it, he advocated *dematerialization,* the desire to eliminate from painting even vestigial representations of natural objects; it was a demand closely paralleling Malevich's ideal of Suprematism, and possibly stemmed from the same Old Russian spiritual sources. Kandinsky's book deeply influenced Klee, even though it was based in large part on Mme Blavatsky's *The Key of Theosophy,* that made the occult a synonym of "eternal truth."[3] As a reaction to the "aimless, nightmarish materialism" of the surrounding culture, Kandinsky demanded that the visual arts turn to the example of music, to "the spark of inner life"—that is, to pure artistic emotion without referent.

◆ ◆ ◆

IN 1914, KLEE TOOK THE PIVOTAL TRIP TO TUNISIA that first sensitized him to the Mediterranean magic. His maternal Arab descent may have impelled him to seek the light and architectures of northern Africa. At Tunis, Carthage, and Kairouan he seemed to get in touch with an ancestral abode. He felt strangely at home there and returned to Europe a changed man. His sense of color was heightened: through the discovery of color, of his "oneness with it," he thought of himself for the first time as a mature painter.

Klee's art is a balance between two extremes: a first level representation, and a second level effects resulting from purely formal treatments. Given the dynamic structure of many of his works, the temptation is great to search for a story, a possible imaginary voyage, the intention of a fable, a confession, or for any narrative at all. And it may be wrong to yield to such a temptation. However, if the inquiry be limited to formal analysis, would that not excise half of the artist's performance which was never purely formal but attempted to remain on the plane of abstract concreteness?

✦ ✦ ✦

THE DRAWING TITLED *RIBBONLIKE TONAL VALUES*, 1915 (pl. 1), is an extraordinary atmospheric piece in black and white, apparently a prototype for other abstract, fantastic architectural compositions to follow. There is a dominance of ribbon forms, such as he used that same year in some of his portraits (e.g. *The Poet-Draftsman* made entirely of bands, where Chagall's influence can be felt, or the better known *Architecture with Red Flag*). Yet the drawing seems to emphasize the planarity of walls, their heaviness, the abstract articulation of volumes; it appears to be about the capacity of heavy objects and coffins to move around as if pushed by secret internal mechanisms, to enclose a space forever, yet to offer, in spite of the final closure, an opening, a ray of hope, an indication of a way out. A small prisonlike window with diagonal bars[4] projects a light; even without indicator-arrows (which occur in later, similar works) one feels that this is the main attractor, the focal point of the journey toward freedom. A number of grey bands in varying tonal values seem to lead to it by means of slow and complicated trajectories that require time from the viewer to be divined. There seems to be an encoded path out of the menacing space where, lacking the cipher, one could be entombed forever. Formally, these straps, transparent bands and ribbons, the folds and scrolls suspended in the air, convey a sense of Cubist stereometry. However, the dreamlike approach, the absence of an object as central focus, the architectural "incoherence" of the visionary eye belie the Cubist analogy.

Transfers from space to time and time to space were central to Klee's conscious aesthetic. In that period, the kinship of music and painting was in the air. Ravel had launched the notion that the laws of harmony were the same for music as for painting. Since Rimbaud and Baudelaire, artists had been on the lookout for correspondences between colors and vowels, and colors and moods. Mallarmé had spoken of the "color of sounds." Cézanne, Gauguin, the Symbolists, Picasso, Kandinsky, each in his own way, were visual musicians. Colors appeared now as the keyboard, the eyes were the hammers, the soul became an instrument with many strings. Colors were endowed with a life of their own. Said Kandinsky: "Some appear soft (rose madder), others hard (cobalt green, green-blue oxide), so that even fresh from the tube they seem to be dry." They certainly were scented and different to the touch. "Vermillion, for example, is a red with a feeling of sharpness." Colors were first of all qualities; secondly, they had weights; thirdly, they could be measured, and so forth. This fantastic effervescence in the theory of colors amounted to a promulgation of the freedom to improvise absolutely, to express without restraint one's inner character and immaterial soul.

Klee was enthusiastic about the idea of the mutual translatability of music and painting. Both he and Kandinsky were convinced that painting should be suffused with musicality. They also were deeply impressed with Robert Delaunay's artistic evolution: first, his revival of decorativism, then Orphism,[5] later still, his and his wife Sonya's development of Simultaneism. This latter theory was unveiled in the circle that gathered around Guillaume Apollinaire, possibly in the spirit of Bergson's *Durée et Simultanéité,* and became for a while the focus of Delaunay's artistic practice. With Delaunay and others, a totally abstract form of art, based on the dynamic properties of pure prismatic colors, was emerging in France. His famous *Windows* series had turned the Cubist scaffolds into transparent colored abstractions. Klee was decidedly under Delaunay's spell. As for Cubism, despite some reservations, Klee absorbed it, creating surfaces that contained layered volumetric perspectives, projections of the multiple views of analytical Cubism.

Klee's watercolors of that period betray his delight in abandoning line and painting with transparent colors of various tonalities, while increasingly deviating from naturalism. His intensive grounding in music theory allowed him to operate with each color as if it were a note and to create a splendidly clear pictorial analog of musical themes.

Around 1920 Klee produces his distinctive flat color rectangles arranged in grids, each of which acts similarly to a musical theme. These constructions are both musical and architectural, and the rectangles may be said to function either as notes or as bricks.

Palace <Red Violet/Yellow Green Diametrical Color Gradation>, 1922 (pl. 4), is a brilliant work resulting from the polyphonic technique of overlapping colored planes. It shows a three-tiered hieratic structure topped by pointed roofs, with a number of asymmetrical windows and niches illumined as from the inside, each containing a candle or other devotional object. To achieve the chromatic gradation with complementary colors, Klee used thinned paint washes, adding transparent layer upon transparent layer at a right angle, achieving thus a double effect: pictorial depth and a totally new set of colors. At a distance, the palace gives the illusion of church music, emanating from an assembly of squares that resemble stained-glass windows; it is a sample of the *inner circle* paintings from the Weimar period. In the early twenties, works achieved with similar techniques carry archetypal titles, such as *Harmony, Sound, Triads, Harmony in Blue and Orange, Harmony of Squares,* and *Intensification of Color From Static to the Dynamic.*

Marjamshausen, 1928 (pl. 15), though a later production, shows the combination of architecture and music in a different version. The painting contains only geometrical figures in vivid yet translucent colors, towering upon each other along invisible vertical grids. Pure color and architectural composition in a vertical plane suggest childlike block construction and a dream city as well.

Turning away from line for more than a short time, however, proved impossible for Klee, as it would have been to throw away his deep personality, his active involvement with abstraction. Linearity and abstraction were mutually conditioned: one can only be abstract with blots and lines, he said, not with colors. Around 1919, he reinstated the linear element to the position it had before 1915: it would function from now on as a balancing element on an equal footing with the color tone blocks.

Klee's line was an intimate synthesis of emotionally contained descriptivism, irony, finesse, drama, pent-up sentiment, and an incessant marveling at the world, of both the senses and the mind. It is a curiously ascetic expression of sensuality. His line can be an arabesque, a concentrate of grace, a rhythmic repetition, an expression of doubt and faith, regret and hope, of steadfastness, obdurateness even. Its fluidity reveals the essential stream of natural and psychological processes. It is a line in search of the "enchanted bridge that would unite the outer cosmos to the inner one."

A Piece of the Moon World, 1917 (pl. 3)—lending its title to the present show— is an eerie work that relies exclusively on the suggestiveness of line and the effect of scattering figures in an abstract space. With *Aquatic Plants, 1917* (pl. 2), of the same year, it belongs to a series of early, "mystical landscapes"[6] composed of cosmic symbols, some of them part of the Bavarian peasant mythology to which Klee was particularly attached. These signs in the sky are disposed in an arbitrary pattern: suns, moons in all phases, especially quarter-moons, six-pointed stars and asterisks but, interestingly enough, an airplane/bird too (it was the middle of WWII), and the word *Mond* (moon) spelled out in script. This sublunar world is drawn and shaded in extremely fine pencil lines.

◆ ◆ ◆

IN HIS *CREATIVE CREDO,* Klee maintains that art does not reproduce the visible, but is a simile, "occasionally an example, of Creation, just as the terrestrial exemplifies the cosmic." Klee sees the work of art as a genesis out of chaos which he conceives, however, not as complete and utter chaos, but as locally determined, relative only to the totality of the cosmos. Klee sought to demonstrate that near chaos, states of order, far from being merely decorative, have a troubling germinative power. He was bent on painting what Spinoza called *natura naturans,* nature in the process of engendering itself, the emergence of ever-new forms, and the artistic rules of this morphogenesis. His approach is totally different from the static *natura naturata* of the Aristotelian still-life objects that students for generations were obliged to copy in academic workshops.

Seeing art only as a simile of Creation, Klee still did not believe that the "wretched light of art" could penetrate beyond the "ultimate circle" of cosmic mysteries; these had to be approached in code as well. Nature eventually reverts to its own secret ciphers that negate our acculturating activity. To our eyes this undoing of cultural codes may look wild and chaotic, but one must at least attempt to read it. This seems to be the general drift of meaning in two later works that exemplify the fine musical balance between nature and culture, as between randomness and order: *Short Story in Secret Code,* 1935 (pl. 33), and *Garden Grown Wild,* 1939 (pl. 32).

Like so many other "semiotic" works, *Short Story in Secret Code* seems to look at a dance of signs through a pictorial lens, arresting thus their mysterious moves and significations. A scattering of half-formed letters, runes, and musical notes, a spiraling shape, a fermata, and other of Klee's favorite symbols are placed in a field of forces, the center of which is an oval vortex. The work is extremely effective in terms of the color contrast between the yellowish background and the salient black ink of the signs. There is a secret harmony of the whole, alluding perhaps to the balance of order and randomness, encoding and decoding, in any artistic creation. The elaborate texture of the background and the fine egg glazing give it particular brilliance.

Garden Grown Wild is a truly minimal work: on a crumpled yellow paper some irregular figures in black chalk are dispersed in an enigmatic inner harmony that would have charmed John Cage. One could say of both these works what Mozart wrote to his father about three of his piano concertos:

> They are . . . exactly between too hard and too easy. Very brilliant, pleasing to the [eye], *naturally without lapsing into emptiness;* here and there only connoisseurs will find satisfaction but in such a way that even non-connoisseurs must feel content without knowing why.[7]

In a similarly minimal but more romantic vein reminiscent of Novalis is *Night of Love,* 1937 (pl. 31), where pastel, gouache, and red colored paste are used jointly on the background of two deep blues, the juxtaposition of which would have seemed impossible to anyone but Klee.

◆ ◆ ◆

TRANSPARENCY, TRANSLUCENCE, AND INTERPENETRATION of colors were things Klee did not invent but only pursued, with variations of his own, within a tradition going back to Leonardo and having its roots in the early glazing techniques and incipient colorism of the Flemish masters. Pictorial polyphony, on the other hand, was virgin land, a pure desire for the sublime, as, for instance, extant in a Mozart concerto or symphony. "This phenomenon of many simultaneous dimensions which helps drama to its climax, does not, unfortunately, occur in the world of verbal didactic expression," wrote Klee in his Jena Lecture of 1923 which could qualify as his *Discourse on Method*.[8] And, later, imparting his theoretical beliefs about form, he declared that he had always concentrated on the "formative powers rather than the finished result":

> The artist as philosopher...must be forgiven if he looks upon the present stage of this...phenomenal world as accidentally caught in space and time, and if it strikes him as absurdly limited compared to the more profound, more mobile world of his vision and feeling.[9]

Because of his emphasis on the fantastic and the visionary, Klee was hailed as a kindred spirit by the Surrealists (Crevel wrote in 1929: "Klee's oeuvre is a complete museum of the dream"), but he did not reciprocate with much enthusiasm. Neither automatism, with its quick recording of images in succession, nor, apparently, psychoanalysis appealed to him; Klee worked slowly and in full lucidity. He did, nevertheless, acknowledge the powers of the unconscious as well as the artistic possibilities of free associations:

> It supplies . . . a key to the fantasy and formal significance of a picture. Within the will to abstraction something appears that has nothing to do with objective reality. It is the 'abstract cosmos.' This world of illusion is credible. It is situated in the realm of the human.[10]

One area, however, where his compositions verge on abstract Surrealism is that of architecture. He used various forms as signs for architectural elements—books, abstract volumes, geometrical shapes, etc.[11] There is a solemn quality in Klee's imaginary architectural objects, as if they were classical temples of unknown rites. They encode and reveal symbols that challenge the eye to travel along their inner paths; and they set the mind and the spirit at rest. This is where Klee crosses the path of Islamic art which is more than a passing influence with him: from the purely decorative to the calligraphic script of Kufi manuscripts to the signs of contemplative faith, there is in Islam a knowledge from within, the cosmic perspective of which he naturally shared.

Klee had dreamt for years of seeing Egypt. The journey came about in 1927 and, although it lasted for less than a fortnight, it left profound impressions that lingered for years to come. The golden sky of Egypt, the extraordinary sight of the mixed cultivated and flooded strips of the Nile country, the mythology, the very spirit of Egypt, *ka,* and finally the monuments and their mysterious, funereal mechanics were not immediately expressed in Klee's work but continued, slowly, to fertilize his imagination.

The jewel-like *Orpheus,* 1929 (pl. 17), is a brilliant watercolor on cotton belonging to Klee's "Egyptian manner." The surface virtually sings in several voices with the glow of horizontal strips in bright greens, yellows, oranges, and reds. These are intersected by two oblique lines that enclose a pyramidal space made of wider strips of contrasting colors and directions. It looks as if this space were an erotic, piercing impulse concentrated in Orpheus's gaze, of which the legend speaks. A mysterious dark "flap," in the upper right corner could allude to the forbidden look back that cost Orpheus the life of Eurydice. While seemingly narrating a myth, the sheer counterpoint of color strips provides enchantment in itself.

◆ ◆ ◆

PARALLEL LINES ARE ONE OF THE MOST DELICATE, idealized, rigorous, and stern modalities of designating (not representing) volumes. Borrowed from cartography, they lovingly envelop the contours of hillocks, rivers, or imaginary objects; they can be drawn at various angles and produce remarkable effects of height, depth, zigzags, and labyrinths. They stand in contrast to the vibrancy and the dilution in the margins of *tachiste* color; they signal abstraction and flow, dynamic precision as opposed to geometric fixity; and they cannot occur together with color unless the meandering is gentle and curvilinear, and the color faint, almost a pastel blush.

This is similarly the case in *Monastery Garden . . . . .,* 1926 (pl. 8), a masterpiece of finery and lacelike sinuous contours; one can read the ascetic bent coupled with a Franciscan rejoicing in flower beds, birds, the sun and the moon—and meekness. The innumerable crisscross paths are an infinite occasion for the wandering eye to dwell, or, taking one tiny step at a time, to meditate on the way.

In the same style, *Unfolding,* 1925 (pl. 9), is a slow ballet of parallel curves, a dance to the score of an "immanent music," adding fold upon fold, in harmonious angles and rhythms, unveiling perhaps a rosebud, perhaps a little face shielded by a hand from the light. This extraordinary drawing (second only to the one entitled *Creator* of 1934, humorously endowed with a catlike face) contains the shadowy figure of a man, perhaps the artist himself. It offers, on the one hand, an extended metaphor of what Klee's style essentially stood for: the careful, melodic constitution of a model of biological motion, of organic growth, on which every other development ought to mold itself. On the other hand, this technique exhibits, according to Walter Ueberwasser, "a miracle of self-control in the twentieth century."

In *Archipelago 2,* 1927 (pl. 11), the pen-and-ink tracing, at once hesitant and determined, fluid and scratchy, seems propelled by the desire to exhaust the relief and the silhouette of a self-enclosed, quasi-horizontal island structure. As we follow the nervous, semi-continuous line, we experience to a heightened degree "the pleasure of a text" being written in quick motion in front of our very eyes; barely above the horizon, like a thread of mist, the Archipelago floats. It is, formally, a minimalist drawing, a lyrical suggestion of the melancholy of insular existence.

◆ ◆ ◆

IN A RELATIVELY RECENT, well-illustrated and, at a certain level, even persuasive, monograph entitled *Klee and Nature,* Richard Verdi rightly claims that Klee's symbiosis with vegetal nature started early in his youth, that plants are his best explored analogies. But Verdi dubiously leaps to the conclusion that even when and if "surrealistically transposed," Klee's art, excepting perhaps architecture,[12] can be reduced to a mixture of fantasies and realism about plants. As evidence he cites *Passionate Plants* (1914), the blossoms of which are accomplished coquettes, and Klee's curiosity about the sexual life of plants (hermaphroditic species, phallic male flowers), or the double status of *Klebsiella* which stands between plant and animal.

Indisputably, botanical morphologies play a major role in Klee's work, but they are no more than signs of Goethe's "growth and metamorphosis" principle, of the harmony in multiplicity that the artist pursued all his life. Verdi's thesis that Klee was a "nature realist" misses the essential point: Klee's declared goal, repeatedly expressed, was to reach to the essence of morphogenesis, to achieve a *formal cosmos,* not an inventory of natural formations. Klee's most central, emphatic pronouncements (like those of Kandinsky, Delaunay, and others) go against Verdi's interpretation. Yes, the artist does not paint the visible; he makes visible. But as a fragment of nature the artist is in constant dialogue with nature and paints it even as he paints himself, his thoughts, his states of mind.

An oil painting, from the North Sea series, titled *Little Dune Picture,* 1926 (pl. 10), is brushed in extremely vivid colors, a serial arrangement of greens and coral oranges, with delicate yet energetic strokes for the harsh grasses. As a view taken from below the dunes, it has a vertical perspective ending at the deep emerald of the sea. It could almost be considered a "nature pole" in Klee's work.

The "metaphysical pole" is embodied in the works of the *inner circle,* among which the *Gaze of Silence*, 1932 (pl. 26), is one of the most remarkable. Paintings, it is said, look at us; sad or smiling, serene or severe, inspiring, reproaching, intense or relaxed, consoling us or frightening us. The eye, unlike any other organ of the body human, is at once seeing and seen. In the *Gaze of Silence*, the eye could be an Egyptian hieroglyph, or it could double as a sun. It emerges in the middle of pastel colored fields, bordered by intersecting curves; only the space enclosing the sun proper is orange, all the others are shades of green. The jute on which the color is applied lends an archaic look. The painting has the fixity of a reminder, something as powerful and obsessive as the Islamic *dikhr*—the (ineffable) memory of God. This eye haunts and possesses you as you walk around in the room; it holds a key of access to spirituality. Plain, of an almost provocative simplicity, centered in that elongated symbolic shape, it has the sparseness and the poignancy of a primitive painting. As in most of Klee's works, the title itself goes a long way towards clarifying the intended meaning. Here it is: a silent eye that gazes, insistent, profound, unblinking. This is one of the great Klee paintings that signify on many levels, including that of the numinous.

◆ ◆ ◆

IT HAS BEEN SAID THAT the mysterious arrows almost ubiquitously present in Klee's works are linked with the passage of time, entropy, decline, the irreversibility of fate. But this is not always the case. The value certainly is more than indexic, as when they show the way out of the labyrinth or point to the opening of a grave, or to a path to be tread upon.

In Untitled *(Vegetation in Rejuvenation)*,1924 (pl. 7), a fine, featherlike array of mosses covers geometric and biomorphic figures. Five arrows of various dimensions, including one explicitly curved clockwise, equally surrounded by hatchings, show the direction of unfolding in the renewal of vegetation in the spring. The direction of the arrows has a double signification: if centrifugal, it indicates unfolding and growth; if centripetal, with a shrinking radius, it points towards death and decay.

Henri Michaux, the French poet who was himself a painter of great delicacy and inspiration, describes thus the manner of Klee's vegetation paintings where arrows occur:

> Thanks to the moving, faint modulations of his colors that do not even seem applied but rather exhaled at the right place, or else naturally rooted as mosses or rare molds, his "tranquil natures" in the fine tonalities of antique things, seemed ripe with age and with a slow organic life, as having come into the world by gradual emanations.[13]

◆ ◆ ◆

23

AT THE BAUHAUS, where Klee spent ten years (Weimar, 1921–28; Dessau, 1928–31) of intense concentration in teaching and clarifying his own theoretical stance, the emphasis was construction and everything related to it: "Building is the culmination of all creative endeavor." Klee took this maxim to heart, but later he began to object to the school's modes of implementing it. He would become a dissenter to the excessive technologization of building processes.

For Klee, architecture was first and foremost a poetical and musical endeavor; one would search in vain for pragmatic validity here. When he did "architecture," Klee would not rest until he has posed ground plan against elevation views. But his "architectons" (to use Malevich's term, which designates a unit and a model rather than a finished, usable plan) are at most an inspiring idea, a hint of atmosphere, a thrust, a line, a contour, or a sample of *style* rather than a working plan.

In some of his architectural drawings, Klee seems formally closer to the Russian Constructivists than the Cubists, even though his artifacts served no social purpose and bore no trace of futuristic enthusiasm or revolutionary rhetoric. Yet his exercises in quiet ecstasy have some similarities with the themes of Malevich, for example: the use of the flat rectangle as energy source, musical analogies (as music consists of two dimensions, pitch and duration, so the painting should be two-dimensional), the advocacy of *dematerialization* as intrinsic to the aesthetic of abstract art. Said Klee: "The immaterial needs no fixed base, it hovers; no simile is possible for it." There may be affinities with El Lissitzky too, definitely with Moholy-Nagy, both of whom had strong links with the Bauhaus in the twenties. Klee often espoused their bold, ascending line and flying geometric figures, perhaps finding in them a parallel to the suspension of traditional values rooted in stability and conformity.

Old High-Rises, 1928 (pl. 14), one of Klee's group of architectural drawings, actually recalls the daring upsurge of Constructivism: glass structures within glass structures, a vertical rhythm, some regular contours of houses topped by regular roofs, shaky ladders strewn about between buildings, as if the whole were still under construction, and ladders that lead to closed spaces or to improbable landings. The occasional semblance of normal perspective is invariably thwarted by the incongruity of anti-perspectival elements.

House of the Opera Buffa, 1925 (pl. 13), is a marvel of style, delicacy, humor, and musical allusions. A fine brush drawing in a faint red color, it is a rather complex two-dimensional rococo building complete with domes, arched windows, balconies, ladders, and musical keys, suggesting perhaps the playful intricacies of Mozart's opera *Così Fan Tutti* (for which Klee wished he had designed the settings).

Although uninterested in classical perspective, Klee sometimes used it, with modifications, as in the aerial perspective of his Egyptian paintings (*Highway and Byways* and *The Nile Delta*) and in the drawing of a *Lived-in Room* of 1921, dating from the Bauhaus period. But mainly he exhibited a keen sense of the other potentialities of space: its vectors, its abrupt shifts of perspective, its fantastic motility leading up to the vortexes that seem to annul all dimensionality.[14] In *Sharp Turns,* 1937 (pl. 29), we are confronted with a conflagration of vectors that sweep us into the gyrating, transparent space of color and beyond. Everything is twisted, giving rise to a strange geometry, or rather a topology, of whirling space. Writes Merleau-Ponty:

> Take topological space as a model of being. The Euclidian space is the model for perspectival being, it is the space without transcendence, positive, a space of straight lines, parallel among themselves or perpendicular according to the three dimensions which sustain all possible situations. . . . The topological space, on the contrary, a milieu in which are circumscribed relations of proximity, of envelopment, etc., is the image of a being that, like Klee's touches of color, is at the same time older than everything, and "of the first day."[15]

Klee's true ambition, however, was to forge a dynamic synthesis between musical and pictorial form. He achieved it through the development of his most original technique, that of "divisionism." Music is indeed the key to many an enigmatic feature of Klee's work of this period. A practicing musician since childhood, he felt that he could contribute in painting something akin to the introduction of counterpoint in music in the eighteenth century. One of his favorite readings was *Gradus ad Parnassum, [Ladder to Parnassus]*, a treatise by the Austrian musician and theoretician Johann Joseph Fux, to which Mozart, Haydn, Beethoven, and, in Klee's time, Hindemith, were indebted. Instrumental counterpoint was a most important element in German music, while French music tended towards monodic, homophonic, or melody-and-accompaniment styles. It is more than likely that Klee's famous *Ad Parnassum* painting of 1932, as well as many formal compositions whose subject matter is less important than their actual surface technique of "polyphonic weaving," refer to Fux's treatise.

Fux believed it was more essential to understand the formative function of each element in the creation of art than to be concerned with the finished form. In the same spirit, Klee was interested—and his courses at the Bauhaus show it—in mathematical rules, acoustical physics, arithmetic and harmonic progressions. He often presented his students with exercises in analytical geometry, trigonometry on a sphere, mechanics, statics, dynamics, and related disciplines in the hope of arriving at a certain scientific foundation for art.

Needless to say, that the finished products of Klee's genius could not be reduced to a single scientific alphabet or set of rules.

The next step was to be decisive by virtue of its complexity and multivalence: it was the introduction proper of polyphony in painting. Divisionism, Klee's way of achieving polyphony in painting using music as a model, is more than a vague analogy: not gratuitous ineffability but a precise, almost quantifiable method. Klee had earlier layered colored themes upon themes, in which his skill at intertwining transparency and opacity had found free expression. But the new technique was a significant step forward.

This so-called pointillism[16] is rather a "counterpointillism": he called it *theory of dividuality,* in contrast to *individuality.* Dividuality is the property of objects to be divisible up to a certain limit, given by a physically achievable unit. The theory, in turn, gave rise to the new technique of divisionism: a monotonous rhythm can be divided into elements that, superimposed on other colored structures, can create a musical, non-monotonous effect of the whole. A fish, as Klee demonstrated in his classes at the Bauhaus, can be seen both 1) as an individual and 2) "dividually." Take the fish as a whole; find a principle of dividing it—for instance, its own scales; make a grid of it; spread this grid over the whole surface of the painting. The fish and its environment will still be visible through the grid, but the whole will be completely and differently "illumined" by the grid. Klee painted little squares or rectangles, colored circles or dots, and sometimes little rectangular mosaics that he superimposed on other object structures, creating something like a dotted veil that gives the illusion of transparency. He was obsessed with transparency and translucence, possibly finding in them an aesthetic correlate of honesty and moral integrity, and with the idea of a seeing-through, a seeing-beyond.

Unlike the pointillism of Impressionists like Seurat, Signac, or, for a short time, Pissarro, which was meant to pulverize, diffuse, or intensify light, divisionism is, in a real sense, another way of "throwing light" on things, by way of concealing the contours of some objects behind the veil of another, more surprising (and perhaps more scientific), atomic truth. Although, like pointillism, divisionism enhances pictorial light, its main function is to *create depth,* and to allow two distinct melodic themes—*one in the background, one in the foreground*—to be carried out simultaneously, with crystalline fluidity. This covering-uncovering, *aletheic*[17] way of approaching truth-in-painting singularly chimes in with the sayings of Heraclitus and Heidegger: it is the nature of nature to hide—and to reveal itself at the same time.

Divisionism remains Klee's most important technical innovation, even though it produced only a few remarkable paintings. Rightly famous were works of the Dessau and Düsseldorf periods, like *Fermata* (1932), *Polyphony,*

Ad Parnassum, and the *Mosaic from Prhun* (1931). In this exhibition, *Two Accented Layers*, 1932 (pl. 27), offers a classical instance of the technique of divisionism. Two strips of plain color, green and brown, contrapuntally interrupt the dotted surface. The general effect is that of a dense weaving; as in a rug—not a tapestry—with a warp and weft, the opaque lines cut the monotony of the dotted surface and energize it. The effect here at first glance is merely decorative. However, there seems to be more to it: a certain transparent uniformity is created, underneath which the real variation of the underlying washes is at once concealed and revealed.

◆ ◆ ◆

IN THE THIRTIES THE BAUHAUS became a hotbed of political and administrative bickering. Johannes Meyer, a Swiss architect who succeeded Walter Gropius as director, was a Marxist who put excessive emphasis on practicality and technical training and stirred up ideological controversy. Klee tried at first to treat the situation with humor, drawing anecdotal scenes about the academic battles. But little by little, he came to rebel against the increasing dominance of technology in the arts. His own course had always been marginalized as "optional" in the curriculum, and its continuation was often threatened in the general economy of the instruction. In September 1930, he submitted to Mies van der Rohe, the new director of the Bauhaus, a formal letter of resignation; the next spring, he left for Düsseldorf. The Bauhaus, twice suspended by the Nazis, and twice reopened, was finally closed in 1933. Later that year, suspended from the Düsseldorf Academy, his house searched by the Nazis, and in imminent danger of arrest, Klee fled with his family to Switzerland. In 1933, Klee and Kandinsky painted for the last time in Germany. Their only sin— "political" indeed—had been abstraction!

A series of works, mainly portraiture, date from the early part of Klee's exile. *Man of Sorrows*, 1933 (pl. 22), is a haunting portrait in red of a man with an oblong face, a small beard, and a mustache, whose huge eyes are in tears, blurred by inordinate suffering. The face itself is deeply furrowed. Whitish, pasted tufts of hair on his forehead and mustache seem now to writhe, now to dangle limp. The expression is one of infinite grief. It is likely that this tragic mask is a result of the trauma inflicted on Klee by his forced exile from Germany: uprooted and disoriented, his creative life had been disrupted for more than half a year. On the other hand, Klee felt protected in Bern and tried not to think too much about what he had left behind. His decision to leave Germany had been irrevocable, and he had no second thoughts: "I would rather accept any amount of personal discomfort than become a tragi-comic figure trying to ingratiate myself with Hitler and his two lion-tamers," he wrote in his diary of that year.

This painting has famous precursors of which two deserve to be mentioned: *Lomolarm [Man in Tears],* a pun on the French *L'homme aux larmes,* and *Child Consecrated to Suffering,* both of 1923. The theme of mankind's suffering was perennial in Klee. In *Man of Sorrows,* the reference to Christ is explicit: it takes on a definitely Christlike connotation. Between 1930 and 1940, the wandering playfulness of the previous drawings appears only episodically. Instead we witness a concentration on archetypes of suffering.

Also from 1933 is *Written in the Face,* 1933 (pl. 23), a little "idiotic" drawing of a moonlike face, as of an alien; the eyes and the nose are intersecting curves, the mouth barely a horizontal dash. The sense of distress and psychological regression is overwhelming. Perhaps one eye is still vigilant, the other seems completely engulfed in the deep mourning of the face. If not for the crucial date, the title, and the signature, this drawing could be dismissed as a child's, a madman's, or as an indifferent scribbling. It is a point where Klee (as, in a formal sense, does Cy Twombly) attains universality by default, speaking of a state of dejection so total that it is barely decipherable. Still humanity remains more triumphant perhaps than in the portraits of Renaissance nobility.

Far from shunning such primitive expressions, Klee cultivated them consciously as part of his modernist aesthetic:

> These are primitive beginnings in art such as one usually finds in ethnographic collections or at home in one's nursery. Do not laugh, reader. Children also have artistic ability and there is wisdom in their having it! The more helpless they are, the more instructive are the examples they furnish us; and they must be preserved from corruption from an early age. Parallel phenomena are provided by the works of the mentally diseased; neither childish behavior nor madness are insulting words here, as they are commonly. All this is to be taken very seriously, more seriously than all the public galleries when it comes to reforming today's art. [18]

Opposed to this rather tragic mood is the "demonic" humor of the thirties. Late in his life, only one year before his death, Klee became acquainted with Brueghel and Bosch, and Goya's *Caprichos;* they all left in him an indelible mark. Their demons! He had suppressed them for decades, without realizing who they were, or what they wanted, yet never ceased trying to exorcise them. They were clearly revealed to him in the icons of the earlier masters. And when they finally surface in the series *Infernal Park,* they do so with a certain bonhomie, actually a lugubrious humor. *Mme Emmer,* 1939 (pl. 35), obviously belongs to this series, where plants, flowers, and human bodies intertwine in monstrous embraces and mutual metamorphoses: a pansy with the face and hands of an angry fetus, a female figure "attempting to become a plant," finally

Mme Emmer herself, ensconced in a giant tumbling of flesh, breasts, and limbs, with mechanical hands, or rather prehensile tools, and a sketchy face, topped by a moon. The drawing is a conglomerate of sensual curves—members, organs, fruit—full of unexpected protuberances that let one guess how the barrier separating plant from beast, from man, or from woman, may be crossed. It seems that Klee arrived at this late time at a free projection of his private hells: in particular the nightmarish involution of humans (especially overweight ones) toward vegetable forms. These drawings stand close to the later Picasso monsters.

Another example of this tragic late humor is the *Maenad of Yore,* 1939 (pl. 36), one in a series of mysterious *Eidola*—icons, metaphysical forays into human typologies that Klee worked at throughout his career. The *Maenad* is composed of only a few lines: fallen wings instead of arms, the navel of a mammal, a bird profile, the round eye of a vindictive ghost, as of a bacchante resurging from the past.

That these and other hellish beings bring death to mind is no surprise. Klee seems indeed to have met his death head-on by reliving and animating his memories. Ever since his ecstatic discovery of color at Kairouan, he had also taught himself a detached attitude toward death, and had found the antidote to it: letting the flow of painting submerge him and carry him where it may. He grew increasingly convinced that death is not an evil, only a passage, another face of the living truth, an opening to the other side. He painted his own *Requiem,* complete with Credo, Sanctus, and Agnus Dei. In 1940, four weeks before his death, he sketched a tragic figure, crowned with thorns, *Ecce.* But the very last painting is a still life with jug and pipe, flowers on a tray, a sun on a black ground, and figurines: nothing out of the ordinary, save for one insert in the left hand corner, a little angel of death.

Klee has barely a precursor and no true progeny, although artists from Jean Dubuffet, Nicolas de Staël, Fritz Hundertwasser, and Roger Bissière to several American painters of the forties betray his more or less direct influence. His impact on contemporaries and later artists is easier to retrace and more ubiquitous than the influences he himself was subject to. Perhaps no other painter in the twentieth century possessed such a capacity for wondering at the world, both inner and outer, or such an ability to translate this sense of wonder into abstract yet accessible terms. Klee's almost childlike immediacy greatly contributed toward making the rigors of modernism acceptable to a still refractory public. Some of his simpler technical devices, of course, are easy to imitate, in structure, if not in atmosphere; but it is impossible not to recognize an authentic Klee icon.

One of his endearing qualities has been called, variously, intimacy and lack of pretension. Many note only his humor which ranged from the ferocious to the gentle to the very subtle. While his works can be approached intuitively, at times they demand painstaking deciphering, which in turn requires duration, and the ability to interpret both their remoteness and the aura of their suggestion.

Yet no matter how often seen or scrutinized by laymen and connoisseurs alike—and no matter how many cheap Klee reproductions adorn the walls of humble bistros—their novelty does not wear away: strikingly fresh in their humanity, at each viewing they elicit the sense of an epiphany.

Far from being facile, Klee's playfulness resembles more the lightheartedness, humor, and elegance of a master in full possession of his means, like Mozart. Both worked for children as well as adults, yet they enjoyed universal acclaim for their whole operatic gamut, from comedy to tragedy.

Under the deceptive simplicity, the clownishness and jocularity, the whims, the easy laughter and frequent tears, the self-irony, the puns, the games of signs and ciphers, lies a philosophical genius struggling with the enigmas of primordial origins, who tried to represent the abstract essence of motion, the limits of human intellect, the fusion of the arts, the passion of mankind.

Tacitly but eloquently, he brings to the fore the role of artists in a time of need, and the *perpetuum mobile* of spirituality.

—Ileana Marcoulesco

1. The rare and fatal disease that afflicted Klee was scleroderma, recognized today as an auto-immune syndrome. First, it produces a thickening and drying out of the skin of the fingers and the face, then invades the mucous surfaces of the mouth and the nose, and finally attacks the arteries and the heart.

2. *Diaries,* 1908, 842. He was pondering "how [van Gogh] came *without a break* from Impressionism and yet created novelty. His line is new and yet very old."

3. Klee was skeptical of theosophy. While reading Rudolf Steiner, he exclaimed: "Theosophy?! What makes me particularly suspicious is their visions of color. Even if no fraud is involved, one is self-deceived. The coloration is unsatisfactory and the allusions to formal composition are downright comical. The numbers are impossible. The simplest equation has more meaning.... Naturally I read only part of the book, because its commonplaces soon made it unpalatable to me" (*Diaries,* IV, 377).

4. Around 1912–13, crosses, diamond shapes, and diagonal bars were symbols often used by the Cubists.

5. Apollinaire gave the name Orphism to a style derived from Cubism, where *color in movement,* played the dominant role. Kupka, Picabia, and Duchamp were also connected with this trend.

6. *Mystical Landscape With Worm in the Ground* is the better known work in this series.

7. Quoted in E. H. Gombrich: *The Sense of Order.* (Oxford: Phaidon Press, 1979), 305; emphasis added.

8. *The Sense of Order,* 305.

9. *Notebooks. Vol. I,* 93.

10. *Notebooks. Vol. I,* 262.

11. He also preferred "absolute" to "abstract" architecture; the latter creates only an illusion of volumes, while the former generates a strange feeling of sacredness in the viewer.

12. David Sylvester entertained a similar viewpoint in an otherwise learned and discerning article on Klee written in the fifties. Sylvester would like to pour all of Klee's diversity into two molds, the organic and the architectural. Yet this categorization is easily overthrown upon examination of Klee's other, intertwined approaches to art: the scriptural, the semiotic, the narratively grotesque, the caricatural, the self-portraits, the purely symbolic, the mixed musical analogies, and, above all, the all-pervading demon of abstraction.

13. Henri Michaux, *Aventures de Lignes,* 14.

14. "Dimensions" for Klee were: upwards, downwards, right, left, and the beyond; he sometimes marked them with arrows. Right and left may be arbitrary, yet not totally so, even as the respective positions, in many a case, have taken on identical form, if not meaning.

15. Maurice Merleau-Ponty, *The Visible and the Invisible,* 210.

16. During the years he had spent in southern France at Porquerolles, under the influence of the Impressionists, Klee had perhaps tried his hand at something like pointillism, but soon he developed his own way of approaching light, objects, and fields of color.

17. From *aletheia,* the oldest Greek term for "truth," meaning an uncovering of hiddenness. It is, in the philosophy of Heidegger, opposed to all subsequent descriptions of truth in Western philosophy, and the most powerful.

18. *Diaries,* 1930, 10–11.

Bibliography

Crone, Rainer and Joseph Leo Koerner. *Paul Klee: Legends of the Sign.* New York: Columbia University Press, 1991.

Fryberger, Betsy. *In Celebration of Paul Klee 1879–1940.* Stanford: Stanford University Press, 1979.

Geelhaar, Christian. *Paul Klee and the Bauhaus.* Greenwich, Ct.: New York Graphic Society, 1973.

_____. *Paul Klee: Life and Work.* Woodbury, N.Y., London, and Toronto: Barron's, 1982.

Glaesemer, Jürgen. *Paul Klee: The Colored Works in the Kunstmuseum Bern.* Translated by Renate Franciscono. Bern: Kornfeld and Cie, 1979.

Gombrich, E. H. *The Sense of Order.* Oxford: Phaidon Press, 1979.

Grohman, Will. *Paul Klee.* Translated by Norbert Guterman. New York: Harry N. Abrams Inc., 1954.

Haxthausen, Charles Werner. *Paul Klee: The Formative Years.* New York and London: Garland Publishing, 1981.

Hofmann, Werner, ed. *Traumlandschaft mit Mond. Sechzehn Farbtafeln.* Frankfurt-am-Main: Insel Verlag, 1964.

Hulton, Nika. *An Approach to Paul Klee.* London: Phoenix House, 1956.

Jordan, Jim M. *Paul Klee and Cubism.* Princeton: Princeton University Press, 1984.

Kagan, Andrew. *Paul Klee/Art & Music.* Ithaca and London: Cornell University Press, 1983.

Kandinsky, Wassily. *Concerning the Spiritual in Art.* Translated by M. T. H. Sadler. New York: Dover Publications, 1977.

Klee, Felix. *Paul Klee: His Life and Work in Documents.* New York: Braziller, 1962.

Klee, Paul. *The Diaries of Paul Klee, 1898–1918.* Edited by Felix Klee. Berkeley: University of California Press, 1964.

_____. "On Modern Art" [the Jena Lecture] in Robert L. Herbert, ed. *Modern Artists on Art.* Englewood Cliffs, N.J.: Prentice Hall, 1964, 74–91.

Lachner, Carolyn, ed. *Paul Klee.* The Museum of Modern Art. New York, 1987.

Merleau-Ponty, Maurice. *The Visible and the Invisible.* Edited by Claude Lefort; translated by Alphonso Lingis. Evanston, Il.: Northwestern University Press, 1968.

Michaux, Henri. "Aventures de lignes." in Will Grohman. *Paul Klee.* Paris: Flinker, 1954.

The Museum of Modern Art. *Paul Klee: Three Exhibitions—1930, 1941, 1949.* New York: Arno Press, 1968.

Nierendorf, Karl, ed. *Paul Klee: Paintings, Watercolors 1913–1939.* Introduction by James J. Sweeney. New York: Oxford University Press, 1941.

Ozenfant, Amédée. *Foundations of Modern Art.* Translated by John Radker. New York: Dover Publications, 1952.

Paul Klee 1879–1940: A Retrospective Exhibition. Solomon R. Guggenheim Museum. New York, 1967.

Paul Klee at the Guggenheim Museum. Solomon R. Guggenheim Museum. New York, 1993.

Renzio, Toni del. "The Late Works of Paul Klee." *Art and Artists* (1974), N° 9, 27–29.

Rewald, Sabine. *Paul Klee. The Berggruen Klee Collection in The Metropolitan Museum of Art.* The Metropolitan Museum of Art. New York, 1985.

Rosenthal, Deborah. "A Transparent World: the Notebooks of Paul Klee," *The New Criterion* (1993) vol. 10, N° 1, 33–38.

Roskill, Mark. *Klee, Kandinsky, and the Thought of Their Time, A Critical Perspective.* Urbana and Chicago: University of Illinois Press, 1992.

San Lazzaro, Gualtieri di and Constance Naubert-Riser, eds. *Klee in the Masterworks.* New York: Portland House, 1988.

Spiller, Jürg, ed. *Paul Klee's Notebooks. Vol. I. The Thinking Eye.* Translated by Ralph Mannheim. London: Lund Humphries, 1961.

Ueberwasser, Walter. *Paul Klee: The Later Work.* Galerie Beyeler. Basel, 1965.

Verdi, Richard. *Klee and Nature.* New York: Rizzoli, 1985.

Whitford, Frank. "The Thinking Eye at Work. Paul Klee's Notebooks." *Times Literary Supplement,* 8 April 1994, 10–11.

1. *Ribbonlike Tonal Values*, 1915

2. *Aquatic Plants,* 1917

3. *A Piece of the Moon World*, 1917

4. *Palace Red Violet / Yellow Green
Diametrical Gradation*, 1922

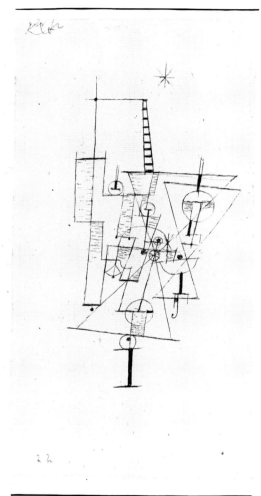

5. *Construction with the Small
Central Wheel*, 1922

6. *The Vocalist*, 1922

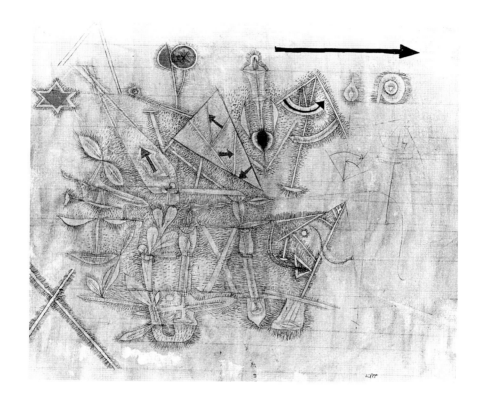

7. Untitled (*Vegetation in Rejuvenation*), 1924

8. *Monastery Garden . . . . ,* 1926

9. *Unfolding*, 1925

10. *Little Dune Picture*, 1926

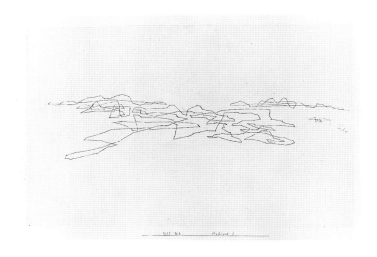

11. *Archipelago 2,* 1927   12. *Fortified Port City,* 1926

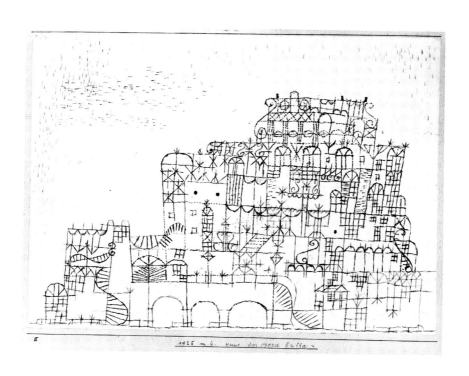

13. *House of the Opera Buffa,* 1925

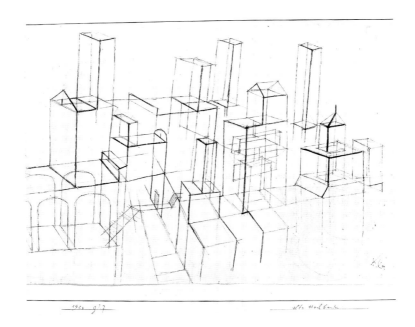

14. *Old High-Rises,* 1928

15. *Marjamshausen,* 1928

16. *Wood Construction for the Stage,*
1929 (Whereabouts unknown)

17. *Orpheus*, 1929

18. *Woman with Bundle,* 1930

930 p.u. Rinde

19. *Bark,* 1930

20. *Adolescents*, 1930

21. *Analysis of a Moment,* 1931

22. *Man of Sorrows*, 1933

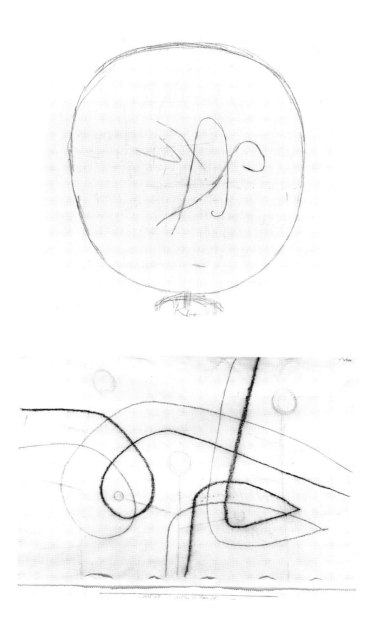

23. *Written in the Face,* 1933   24. *Blossoms in their Place,* 1935

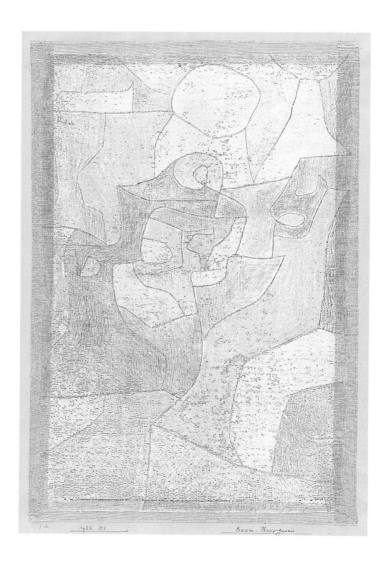

25. *Tree-Physiognomy*, 1932

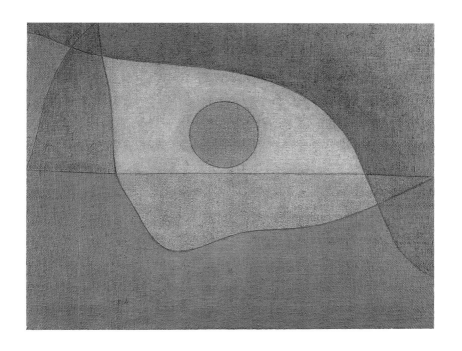

26. *Gaze of Silence,* 1932

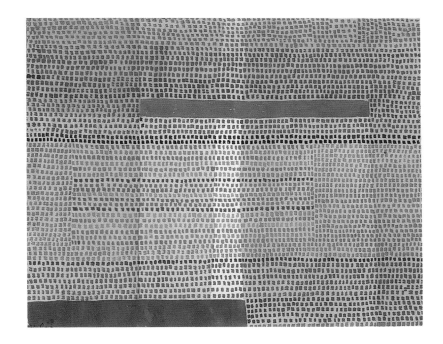

27. *Two Accented Layers*, 1932

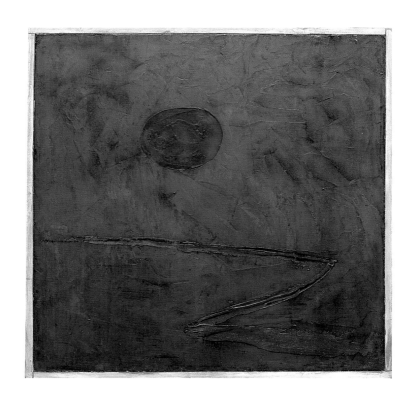

28. *Way into the Blue*, 1934

29. *Sharp Turns*, 1937

30. *Still Life in Brown*, 1937

31. *Night of Love*, 1937

32. *Garden Grown Wild*, 1939

33. *Short Story in Secret Code*, 1935

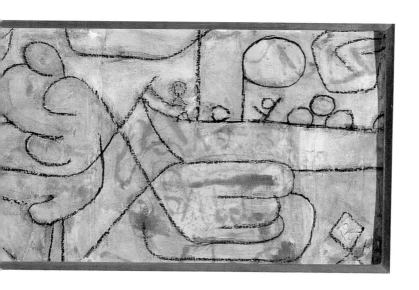

34. *On the River*, 1939

35. *Mme Emmer*, 1939

36. *Eidola: Maenad of Yore*, 1940

List of Illustrations

For almost all his artworks Klee recorded the date, catalogue number, title, technique, color components, and paper type in his Oeuvre Catalogue. Beginning in February 1911 and retroactively including works he considered of merit dating back to 1893, Klee meticulously maintained his catalogue until one month before his death on June 29, 1940. He did not record his works daily but waited until he had collected a group of about ten, disregarding the precise chronology of works within a given group or within a particular year. He started by numbering the works executed each year beginning with one, but from 1925 on he used a combination of letters and numbers. The number following the date identifies the work's chronological position within that year as recorded in his Oeuvre Catalogue (this number is often inscribed on the cardboard mount of works executed prior to 1925). The parenthetical letter and number listed from 1925 on are those inscribed on the cardboard mount.

Klee glued all his works on paper to a secondary cardboard support; this support is accepted as an integral part of the work. In most cases Klee inscribed the title below the image in black ink above or below a marginal line he drew on this support. Sometimes he recorded the title only in his Oeuvre Catalogue, omitting it from the work. The title on a work also might differ somewhat from that in the Oeuvre Catalogue.

The penciled notations "S.Kl." or "S.Cl." *(Sonderklasse)* denote works Klee especially liked. Similarly, the penciled Roman numerals refer to a price system he established for his works in 1925; I represents the lowest price and X the highest. German titles listed are the artist's and have been brought into conformity with modern German orthography. Measurements of works mounted on cardboard include only the image. Dimensions are given in inches followed by centimeters; height precedes width. All data have been confirmed with the Paul Klee Foundation, Kunstmuseum Bern.

FIGURES

fig. 1 *Landschaft*, 1917
[Landscape]
Ink over pencil on writing paper
mounted on cardboard
4 x 6 1/2 in (10.2 x 16.5 cm)
Klee Oeuvre Catalogue: 1917, 151
Collection of Mr. and Mrs.
James M. Vaughn, Jr.

fig. 2 *Strenge Felsbildung*, 1927
[Austere Rock Formation]
Pencil on sketch paper mounted on
cardboard
9 1/8 x 13 in (23.2 x 33 cm)
Klee Oeuvre Catalogue: 1927, 321 (3.H.21)
The Menil Collection, Houston
* *Not in exhibition*

PLATES

1. *bandartig, Tonwerte mit dem* ~~XXXX~~, 1915
[Ribbonlike Tonal Values]
Watercolor washes over pencil on Fabriano
paper mounted on cardboard
5 5/8 x 8 5/8 in (13.5 x 21.9 cm)
Klee Oeuvre Catalogue: 1915, 193
Collection of Janie C. Lee, Houston

2. *Wasserpflanzen*, 1917
[Aquatic Plants]
Pencil on linen paper mounted on
cardboard
3 7/8 x 7 5/8 in (9.9 x 19.3 cm)
Klee Oeuvre Catalogue: 1917, 60
The Menil Collection, Houston

3. *Ein Stück Mondwelt*, 1917
[*A Piece of the Moon World*]
Pencil on linen paper mounted on
cardboard
$7^5/_8$ x $5^1/_2$ in (19.4 x 14 cm)
Klee Oeuvre Catalogue: 1917, 82
The Menil Collection, Houston

4. *Palast <rot violett /*
gelbgrüne Diametral Stufung>, 1922
[*Palace <Red Violet / Yellow Green*
Diametrical Gradation>]
Watercolor washes over pencil on Canson
paper mounted on cardboard with painted
borders
$10^1/_8$ x $11^3/_4$ in (25.7 x 30 cm)
Klee Oeuvre Catalogue: 1922, 65
The Menil Collection, Houston

5. *Konstruction mit dem*
Centralrädchen, 1922
[*Construction with the Small Central*
Wheel]
Ink on German Ingres paper mounted on
cardboard
$9^5/_8$ x $4^7/_8$ in (24.4 x 12.5 cm)
Klee Oeuvre Catalogue: 1922, 225
The Menil Collection, Houston

6. *AAA-Sänger*, 1919
[*The Vocalist*]
Ink on writing paper mounted on cardboard
$11^3/_8$ x $5^{13}/_{16}$ in (28.9 x 14.7 cm)
Klee Oeuvre Catalogue: 1919, 20
The Mary and Sylvan Lang Collection,
McNay Art Museum, San Antonio

7. Untitled *(Vegetation in Rejuvenation)*,
1924
Watercolor and ink on sketch paper
mounted on cardboard
$11^1/_8$ x $12^5/_{16}$ in (28.2 x 32.9 cm)
Klee Oeuvre Catalogue: 1924, 77
The Mary and Sylvan Lang Collection,
McNay Art Museum, San Antonio

8. *Garten des Ordens.....*, 1926
[*Monastery Garden.....*]
Watercolor over ink on writing paper
mounted on cardboard
$8^5/_8$ x $4^3/_4$ in (21.9 x 12.1 cm)
Klee Oeuvre Catalogue: 1926, 21 (L 1)
Private collection

9. *Entfaltung*, 1925
[*Unfolding*]
Ink on German Ingres paper mounted on
cardboard
$12^1/_8$ x $8^1/_4$ in (30.7 x 21 cm)
Klee Oeuvre Catalogue: 1925, 242 (Y 2)
The Menil Collection, Houston

10. *Kleines Dünenbild*, 1926
[*Little Dune Picture*]
Oil on black casein ground on board
$12^7/_8$ x $9^7/_8$ in (32.7 x 25.1 cm)
Klee Oeuvre Catalogue: 1926, 115 (B 5)
The Menil Collection, Houston

11. *Archipel 2*, 1927
[*Archipelago 2*]
Ink on German Ingres paper mounted on
cardboard
$11^5/_8$ x 18 in (29.5 x 45.7 cm)
Klee Oeuvre Catalogue: 1927, 202 (U 2)
The Menil Collection, Houston

12. *Hafen Stadt mit Burg*, 1926
[*Fortified Port City*]
Ink on writing paper mounted on cardboard
$4^1/_2$ x $11^1/_4$ in (11.4 x 28.6 cm)
Klee Oeuvre Catalogue: 1926, 228 (W 8)
The Menil Collection, Houston

13. *Haus der Opera buffa*, 1925
[*House of the Opera Buffa*]
Watercolor on chalk-primed paper mounted
on cardboard
$9^1/_2$ x 12 in (24.1 x 30.4 cm)
Klee Oeuvre Catalogue: 1925, 36 (M 6)
Collection of R.L.B. Tobin

14. *alte Hochbauten*, 1928
[Old High-Rises]
Ink over charcoal on German Ingres paper
mounted on cardboard
9 1/8 x 12 3/4 in (23.2 x 32.4 cm)
Klee Oeuvre Catalogue: 1928, 167 (G 7)
The Menil Collection, Houston

15. *Marjamshausen*, 1928
Watercolor on etching paper mounted on
cardboard with painted borders
14 3/16 x 8 1/16 in (37.9 x 20.3 cm)
Klee Oeuvre Catalogue: 1928, 54 (O 4)
The Museum of Fine Arts, Houston;
gift of Miss Ima Hogg

16. *Holzconstruction für die Bühne*, 1929
[Wood Construction for the Stage]
Ink on Canson paper mounted on cardboard
14 x 8 1/8 in (35.6 x 20.6 cm)
Klee Oeuvre Catalogue: 1929, 53 (O 3)
Whereabouts unknown
* Not in exhibition

17. *Orpheus*, 1929
Watercolor over pencil on cotton fabric
mounted on wood
19 3/4 x 9 1/2 in (50.2 x 24.2 cm)
Klee Oeuvre Catalogue: 1929, 257 (Z 7)
An anonymous lady

18. *die Frau mit dem Bündel*, 1930
[Woman with Bundle]
Colored pencil and incised lines on sketch
paper mounted on cardboard
11 1/4 x 8 1/4 in (28.6 x 21 cm)
Klee Oeuvre Catalogue: 1930, 29 (L 9)
The Menil Collection, Houston

19. *Rinde*, 1930
[Bark]
Colored paste and pencil on German Ingres
paper mounted on cardboard
9 x 12 in (27 x 30.4 cm)
Klee Oeuvre Catalogue: 1930, 70 (P 10)
The Menil Collection, Houston

20. *Jugendliche*, 1930
[Adolescents]
Crayon and pencil on writing paper
mounted on cardboard
11 x 8 1/4 in (28 x 21 cm)
Klee Oeuvre Catalogue: 1930, 106 (U 6)
The Menil Collection, Houston

21. *Analyse eines Momentes*, 1931
[Analysis of a Moment]
Ink over pencil on sketch paper mounted on
cardboard
12 7/8 x 8 1/4 in (32.8 x 21 cm)
Klee Oeuvre Catalogue: 1931, 24 (qu 4)
The Menil Collection, Houston
* Not in exhibition

22. *ein Mann der Schmerzen*, 1933
[Man of Sorrows]
Colored paste on bond paper mounted on
cardboard
13 x 8 1/4 in (33 x 21 cm)
Klee Oeuvre Catalogue: 1933, 405 (F 5)
Private collection, Dallas

23. *ins Gesicht geschrieben*, 1933
[Written in the Face]
Crayon on Detail paper mounted on
cardboard
12 1/4 x 12 3/4 in (31.1 x 32.4 cm)
Klee Oeuvre Catalogue: 1933, 69 (N 9)
The Menil Collection, Houston

24. *Blüten an ihrem Ort*, 1935
[Blossoms in their Place]
Crayon on Detail paper mounted on cardboard
11 5/8 x 16 1/2 in (29.5 x 41.9 cm)
Klee Oeuvre Catalogue: 1935, 85 (N 5)
The Menil Collection, Houston

25. *Baum-Physiognomie*, 1932
[Tree-Physiognomy]
Crayon on plaster-primed gauze mounted
on cardboard
22 1/8 x 15 1/2 in (56.2 x 39.4 cm)
Klee Oeuvre Catalogue: 1932, 266 (H 6)
The Menil Collection, Houston

26. *Blick der Stille*, 1932
[*Gaze of Silence*]
Oil on jute
$21\,^{7}/_{8}$ x $27\,^{3}/_{4}$ in (55.6 x 70.5 cm)
Klee Oeuvre Catalogue: 1932, 285 (Y 5)
The Menil Collection, Houston

27. *zwei betonte Lagen*, 1932
[*Two Accented Layers*]
Gouache and watercolor washes on Italian
Ingres paper mounted on cardboard
$9\,^{3}/_{4}$ x 12 in (24.8 x 30.4 cm)
Klee Oeuvre Catalogue: 1932, 6
The Menil Collection, Houston

28. *Der Weg ins Blaue*, 1934
[*Way into the Blue*]
Encaustic on plywood in original frame
$16\,^{1}/_{4}$ x $16\,^{1}/_{2}$ in (41.3 x 41.9 cm)
Klee Oeuvre Catalogue: 1934, 203 (U 3)
Old Jail Art Center, Albany, Texas;
gift of Bill Bomar

29. *harte Wendungen*, 1937
[*Sharp Turns*]
Colored paste on canvas mounted on
cardboard
$8\,^{3}/_{4}$ x $9\,^{7}/_{8}$ in (22 x 25.2 cm), irregular
Klee Oeuvre Catalogue: 1937, 68 (M 8)
The Menil Collection, Houston;
gift of Pierre Schlumberger

30. *Stilleben in Braun*, 1937
[*Still Life in Brown*]
Oil pastel on paper mounted on cardboard
$11\,^{9}/_{16}$ x $8\,^{1}/_{8}$ in (29.3 x 20.6 cm)
Klee Oeuvre Catalogue: 1937, 174 (S 14)
The Museum of Fine Arts, Houston;
gift of Mr. and Mrs. Pierre Schlumberger

31. *Nacht der Liebe*, 1937
[*Night of Love*]
Colored paste and pastel on gouache painted
paper mounted on cardboard
$13\,^{1}/_{4}$ x $17\,^{1}/_{2}$ in (33.7 x 44.4 cm)
Klee Oeuvre Catalogue: 1937, 21
Collection of Francesco Pellizzi

32. *Verwilderter Garten*, 1939
[*Garden Grown Wild*]
Crayon and ink on thin packing paper
mounted on cardboard
$19\,^{1}/_{4}$ x $10\,^{7}/_{8}$ in (48.9 x 27.6 cm), irregular
Klee Oeuvre Catalogue: 1939, 9
Collection of Christophe de Menil

33. *Novelle in Geheimschrift*, 1935
[*Short Story in Secret Code*]
Watercolor on chalk-primed Ingres paper
$18\,^{15}/_{16}$ x $12\,^{7}/_{16}$ in (48.1 x 31.6 cm)
Klee Oeuvre Catalogue: 1935, 54 (L 14)
Collection of R.L.B. Tobin

34. *Am Strom*, 1939
[*On the River*]
Watercolor and crayon on cotton fabric
mounted on wood in original frame
$8\,^{3}/_{8}$ x $25\,^{5}/_{8}$ in (21.3 x 65.1 cm)
Klee Oeuvre Catalogue: 1939, 353 (Y 13)
Bequest of Marion Koogler McNay, McNay
Art Museum, San Antonio
* *Not in exhibition*

35. *Mme Emmer*, 1939
Pencil on writing paper mounted on
cardboard
$11\,^{3}/_{4}$ x $8\,^{1}/_{4}$ in (29.8 x 21 cm)
Klee Oeuvre Catalogue: 1939, 179 (P 19)
The Menil Collection, Houston

36. *Eidola: Weiland Maenade*, 1940
[*Eidola: Maenad of Yore*]
Pencil on sketch paper mounted on
cardboard
$19\,^{3}/_{4}$ x $13\,^{3}/_{4}$ in (50.1 x 35.1 cm)
Klee Oeuvre Catalogue: 1940, 84 (V 4)
The Menil Collection, Houston

Chronology

1879	Born December 18 in Münchenbuchsee, outside Bern, Switzerland.
1898	Enrolls in Heinrich Knirr's drawing school, Munich.
1900	Enrolls in Munich Academy; studies under Franz Stuck.
1901	Travels in Italy with sculptor Hermann Halle.
1902–06	Lives in Bern.
1906	Moves to Munich. Exhibits *Inventions*, a series of grotesque etchings, in Munich Secession. Marries pianist Lily Stumpf.
1907	Birth of son, Felix.
1908	Produces first oil paintings. Exhibits in Munich and Berlin Secession.
1910	Solo exhibition, Kunstmuseum Bern, and subsequent tour.
1911	Begins cataloguing his works in Oeuvre Catalogue. Exhibits in Galerie Thannhauser, Munich. Illustrates Voltaire's *Candide*, published in 1920. Meets Wassily Kandinsky and August Macke; joins *Blaue Reiter* group.
1912	Exhibits in second *Blaue Reiter* exhibition, Galerie Hans Goltz, Munich. Travels to Paris; visits Robert Delaunay's studio.
1913	Translates Delaunay's essay "La Lumière," published in *Der Sturm*. Exhibits in "Erster deutscher Herbstsalon," Galerie Der Sturm, Berlin.
1914	Founds New Munich Secession with Wilhelm Hausenstein. Travels to Tunisia; discovers color and begins to work mainly in watercolor.
1916–18	Military service in German army.
1919	Rents studio, Schloß Suresnes, Munich. Visits Zurich; makes contact with DADA group.
1920	Retrospective exhibition, Galerie Hans Goltz, Munich. Formally appointed to Staatliche Bauhaus faculty, Weimar. Publication of first monographs on Klee by Leopold Zahn and Hans von Wedderkop.

1923	Visits Kurt Schwitters and El Lissitzky in Hannover.
1924	First solo exhibition in America, Société Anonyme, New York. Delivers lecture "On Modern Art," Kunstverein Jena; published 1945. Establishment of *Die Blaue Vier* by Galka Scheyer.
1925	Bauhaus reopens in Dessau. Establishment of Klee Gesellschaft by Otto Ralfs. Establishes pricing system for past and present works. Exhibits in Surrealist group exhibition, Galerie Pierre, Paris. Publishes *Pädagogisches Skizzenbuch*, Bauhaus-Bücher series (no. 2).
1926	Exhibits in "The Blue Four" exhibition, The Oakland Gallery, California.
1928	Publishes "Exact Investigations in the Realm of Art," *Zeitschrift für Gestaltung.* Travels to Egypt.
1929	Exhibitions in Berlin, Düsseldorf, Dresden, and Paris, honoring fiftieth birthday.
1930	Solo exhibition at The Museum of Modern Art, New York.
1931	Joins faculty of Düsseldorf Academy as Professor of Painting.
1933	Labeled a "degenerate artist" and suspended from Düsseldorf Academy after Hitler assumes power. Returns to Bern.
1935	Retrospective exhibition, Kunsthalle Bern.
1936	Diagnosed with scleroderma.
1937	Included in "Entartete Kunst [Degenerate Art]" exhibition, Munich: 102 works confiscated from German public collections by Nazis.
1938	First exhibitions at Curt Valentin's Buchholz Gallery and Nierendorf's Gallery, New York.
1939	Applies second time for Swiss citizenship; conferred after his death.
1940	Exhibits late work, Kunsthaus Zurich. Dies June 29 in Hospital Sant' Agnese, Muralto-Locarno, Switzerland.

PHOTOGRAPHY

Courtesy of the Josef Albers Foundation, Inc.
Frontispiece and Back Cover

Hickey & Robertson, Houston
pls. 1, 4, 9, 10, 11, 19, 20, 25, 26

George Hixson, Houston
fig. 1; pls. 28, 29

Robert E. Mates, New York
pl. 31, 32

Allan Mewbourn, Houston
pls. 2, 5, 23

O.E. Nelson, New York
pl. 8

John D. Schiff, New York
pl. 16

F.W. Seiders, Houston
fig. 2; pls. 3, 14, 18, 36

Taylor & Dull, New York
pl. 35

Janet Woodard, Houston
pls. 21, 24

All other photographs courtesy of the owners.

Design: Don Quaintance, Public Address Design
Production Assistant: Elizabeth Frizzell
Typography: composed in Stempel Garamond
Color Separations: System Repro, Bonlanden, Germany
Printing & binding: Dr. Cantz'sche Druckerei, Ostfildern, Germany